BEGINNING HIS

FAMILY LIFE
IN WORLD WAR II

009

Gary Patrick

Illustrated by James Field

BEGINNING HISTORY

The Age of Exploration
The American West
Crusaders
Egyptian Farmers
Egyptian Pyramids
Family Life in World War II
Greek Cities
The Gunpowder Plot
Medieval Markets
Norman Castles

Plague and Fire
Roman Cities
Roman Soldiers
Saxon Villages
Tudor Sailors
Tudor Towns
Victorian Children
Victorian Factory Workers
Viking Explorers
Viking Warriors

All words that appear in **bold** are explained in the glossary on page 22.

Series Editor: Deborah Elliott
Book Editor: James Kerr
Designer: Helen White

First published in 1991 by Wayland (Publishers) Limited
61 Western Road, Hove, East Sussex, BN3 1JD.

British Library Cataloguing in Publication Data
Patrick, Gary
Family life in World War II.
1. Great Britain. Social life, 1936–1945
I. Title   II. Series
941.084

HARDBACK ISBN 0–7502–0047–2

PAPERBACK ISBN 0–7502–0923–2

Typeset by Kalligraphic Design, Horley, Surrey.
Printed in Italy by G. Canale & C.S.p.A., Turin.
Bound in Belgium by Casterman, S.A.

CONTENTS

WHAT WAS THE SECOND WORLD WAR?

On 3 September 1939, Britain went to war with Germany. The German leader, **Adolf Hitler**, had used his soldiers to **invade** countries in Europe. The British Government was afraid that Britain might be next on the list.

Most families heard the news on the radio. There was no TV in those days. Many people were afraid because they knew that men would have to go away and fight. They were also warned that their homes might be bombed.

With the threat of German bombing raids, children had to learn how to use gas masks.

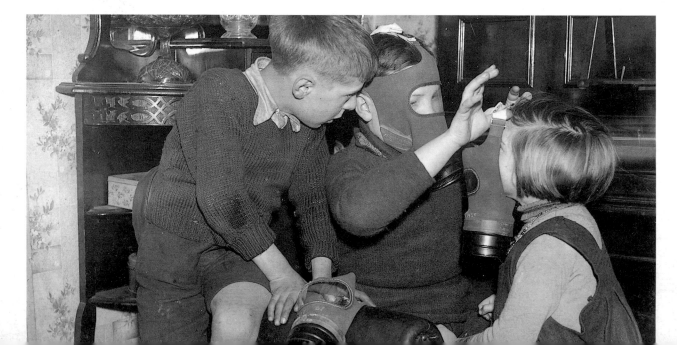

FAMILIES IN THE BLITZ

In 1940 and 1941 the Germans sent aircraft to bomb Britain. London was attacked the most often. This series of air raids was known as **the Blitz**. Air raid wardens made sure that no lights could be seen in houses and streets at night. This was to stop German pilots from seeing where to drop their bombs.

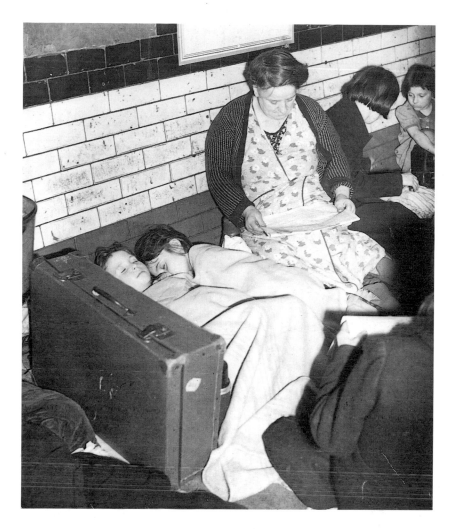

Opposite page, top *Two air raid wardens.*

Opposite page, bottom *London during the Blitz.*

Left *Families in London often slept in the Underground during air raids.*

When the sirens were sounded warning people of an air raid, they went to air raid shelters. Families would listen to the bangs, hoping that their houses had not been hit and that no one they knew had been killed or injured. People kept their spirits up by telling stories and jokes, or singing.

EVACUATION

Children waiting to be evacuated.

Children from towns were sent to the countryside because of the bombing. This was called **evacuation**. Mothers saw their sons and daughters off at railway stations. Sometimes, whole schools of children travelled with their teachers.

Children would arrive in strange places and be sent to live with people they had never seen before. Some children were so unhappy that their mothers took them back home. However, many were happy living in the countryside, which they had never seen before.

SCHOOLS

Some children did not go to school for five years. This was because lots of schools in cities were bombed. It was very hard for village schools to take all of the evacuated children. Because of the extra numbers, children took it in turns to go to school. However, many children did not miss much time at school because some stayed open all through the summer.

A bomb crater in a school playground.

Evacuated children having lessons.

Many male teachers joined the Army, Navy or Air Force. Most teachers in the war were women or old men. There was very little paper and few pencils, so children often worked with chalk and **slates**.

RATIONS

Posters encouraged people not to waste food (**above**). Petrol was also rationed (**below**). *Can you see the ration book?*

Many ships bringing food to Britain were sunk by German submarines. To make sure that everyone had enough to eat, families were given ration books. Every time a family bought something such as meat, the shopkeeper tore a **coupon** out of the book. They were not allowed to buy any more meat until the next week. Clothes were also rationed so people had to make do with their old clothes. If they got damaged, they had to be mended.

Although children still had sweets during the war, they rarely saw fruit from overseas, such as oranges or bananas.

An example of one week's rations of food for one person.

Mothers and Fathers

Some mothers spent the war at home looking after their children. Women whose children had been evacuated often worked in factories, making weapons. Some drove buses or trams. There were lots of jobs to do because men were away fighting.

Not all fathers were away fighting. Many did jobs such as coal-mining. Weapons factories could not operate without coal. Millions of children rarely saw their fathers during the war. Some didn't see them for nearly six years and many fathers never returned.

A woman working in a factory as a welder.

Dad's Army

Even grandfathers wanted to help in the war effort. They worked as air raid wardens and special constables, and they turned every spare patch of land into a vegetable garden.

Above *This 99 year-old man helped in the war effort by growing vegetables.*

Right *A Home Guard regiment training during their lunch break.*

16

The Home Guard guarded important buildings, such as those in London.

Many of them joined the **Home Guard**. This became known as 'Dad's Army', because some of the members were so old. The oldest member was over 80. Their job was to help the Army fight the Germans if they invaded. In the meantime, they trained, guarded important buildings and waited for German **paratroops**. However, the Germans never invaded Britain.

SINGLE WOMEN

These women were ambulance drivers.

Girls and women over eighteen who were not married had to go and work wherever the government ordered them. They would sometimes live with families. More often, they lived in rooms or barns, with many other single women.

Some were told to join the women's
sections of the Army, Navy or Air
Force. Some were sent to work in
factories, or to build ships. Others
joined the **Women's Land Army**
and worked on farms. Most found
themselves in jobs they would never
have dreamed of doing before
the war.

PEACE AT LAST

Although there was hard work and sadness during the war, people managed to stay cheerful. There were comedy shows on the radio, and many people went to dances and to the cinema.

Even so, most people couldn't wait for the war to end. When the Germans surrendered in 1945, the whole country celebrated with huge street parties. The evacuees returned home and troops came back from overseas. Imagine the joy and the tears. Families started to get back to normal. Everybody hoped they would never live through another war.

Schoolchildren at a Victory tea party.

GLOSSARY

Blitz, the The name given to German air attacks on Britain between 1940 and 1941.

Coupon A ticket.

Evacuation Moving from a place of danger to a place of safety.

Hitler, Adolf The leader of Germany between 1933 and 1945.

Home Guard Men who were too old to join the regular Army joined this part-time force.

Invade To send an army into another country by force.

Paratroops Soldiers who jump out of aeroplanes by using parachutes.

Slates Pieces of flat, black stone on which you can write with chalk.

Women's Land Army Women joined this to work on farms.

BOOKS TO READ

The Battle of Britain by Ann Tilbury (Macdonald, 1981)

A Family in World War II by Stewart Ross (Wayland, 1985)

The Home Front by J. F. Aylett (Edward Arnold, 1988)

World War II by Robert Hoare (Macdonald, 1973)

INDEX

Picture acknowledgements

The publishers would like to thank the following for providing the photographs in this book: Camera Press Limited 6 (bottom); The Hulton Picture Library 4, 7, 11, 12 (bottom), 14, 16 (bottom), 17, 18; The Topham Picture Library 6 (top), 8, 10, 12 (top), 13, 16 (top), 21.